MY NOTES

MY NOTES

MY NOTES

MY NOTES

MY NOTES

Calendar 2022

JANUARY

S	M	T	W	T	F	S
26	27	28	29	30	31	1
2	3	4	5	6	7	8
9	10	11	12	13	14	15
16	17	18	19	20	21	22
23	24	25	26	27	28	29
30	31	1	2	3	4	5

FEBRUARY

S	M	T	W	T	F	S
30	31	1	2	3	4	5
6	7	8	9	10	11	12
13	14	15	16	17	18	19
20	21	22	23	24	25	26
27	28	1	2	3	4	5
6	7	8	9	10	11	12

MARCH

S	M	T	W	T	F	S
27	28	1	2	3	4	5
6	7	8	9	10	11	12
13	14	15	16	17	18	19
20	21	22	23	24	25	26
27	28	29	30	31	1	2
3	4	5	6	7	8	9

APRIL

S	M	T	W	T	F	S
27	28	29	30	31	1	2
3	4	5	6	7	8	9
10	11	12	13	14	15	16
17	18	19	20	21	22	23
24	25	26	27	28	29	30
1	2	3	4	5	6	7

MAY

S	M	T	W	T	F	S
1	2	3	4	5	6	7
8	9	10	11	12	13	14
15	16	17	18	19	20	21
22	23	24	25	26	27	28
29	30	31	1	2	3	4
5	6	7	8	9	10	11

JUNE

S	M	T	W	T	F	S
29	30	31	1	2	3	4
5	6	7	8	9	10	11
12	13	14	15	16	17	18
19	20	21	22	23	24	25
26	27	28	29	30	1	2
3	4	5	6	7	8	9

JULY

S	M	T	W	T	F	S
26	27	28	29	30	1	2
3	4	5	6	7	8	9
10	11	12	13	14	15	16
17	18	19	20	21	22	23
24	25	26	27	28	29	30
31	1	2	3	4	5	6

AUGUST

S	M	T	W	T	F	S
31	1	2	3	4	5	6
7	8	9	10	11	12	13
14	15	16	17	18	19	20
21	22	23	24	25	26	27
28	29	30	31	1	2	3
4	5	6	7	8	9	10

SEPTEMBER

S	M	T	W	T	F	S
28	29	30	31	1	2	3
4	5	6	7	8	9	10
11	12	13	14	15	16	17
18	19	20	21	22	23	24
25	26	27	28	29	30	1
2	3	4	5	6	7	8

OCTOBER

S	M	T	W	T	F	S
25	26	27	28	29	30	1
2	3	4	5	6	7	8
9	10	11	12	13	14	15
16	17	18	19	20	21	22
23	24	25	26	27	28	29
30	31	1	2	3	4	5

NOVEMBER

S	M	T	W	T	F	S
30	31	1	2	3	4	5
6	7	8	9	10	11	12
13	14	15	16	17	18	19
20	21	22	23	24	25	26
27	28	29	30	1	2	3
4	5	6	7	8	9	10

DECEMBER

S	M	T	W	T	F	S
27	28	29	30	1	2	3
4	5	6	7	8	9	10
11	12	13	14	15	16	17
18	19	20	21	22	23	24
25	26	27	28	29	30	31
1	2	3	4	5	6	7

CONTACT LIST

Name		Company	
Email		Phone	
Address			
Notes			

Name		Company	
Email		Phone	
Address			
Notes			

Name		Company	
Email		Phone	
Address			
Notes			

Name		Company	
Email		Phone	
Address			
Notes			

Name		Company	
Email		Phone	
Address			
Notes			

PRODUCTIVITY PLANNER

WAKE TIME

_____

TODAY'S MANTRA

_____

SCHEDULE

Time	
8:00	_____
9:00	_____
10:00	_____
11:00	_____
12:00	_____
13:00	_____
14:00	_____
15:00	_____
16:00	_____
17:00	_____
18:00	_____
19:00	_____
20:00	_____
21:00	_____
22:00	_____
23:00	_____

TOP PRIORITIES

- ☐ _____
- ☐ _____
- ☐ _____

TO-DO LIST

- ☐ _____
- ☐ _____
- ☐ _____
- ☐ _____
- ☐ _____
- ☐ _____
- ☐ _____
- ☐ _____
- ☐ _____
- ☐ _____
- ☐ _____

MEMO

DAILY REFLECTION

PRODUCTIVITY PLANNER

WAKE TIME

_____

SCHEDULE

8:00 _____

9:00 _____

10:00 _____

11:00 _____

12:00 _____

13:00 _____

14:00 _____

15:00 _____

16:00 _____

17:00 _____

18:00 _____

19:00 _____

20:00 _____

21:00 _____

22:00 _____

23:00 _____

MEMO

TODAY'S MANTRA

_____

TOP PRIORITIES

☐ _____

☐ _____

☐ _____

TO-DO LIST

☐ _____

☐ _____

☐ _____

☐ _____

☐ _____

☐ _____

☐ _____

☐ _____

☐ _____

☐ _____

☐ _____

DAILY REFLECTION

PRODUCTIVITY PLANNER

WAKE TIME

_____

SCHEDULE

8:00 _____

9:00 _____

10:00 _____

11:00 _____

12:00 _____

13:00 _____

14:00 _____

15:00 _____

16:00 _____

17:00 _____

18:00 _____

19:00 _____

20:00 _____

21:00 _____

22:00 _____

23:00 _____

TODAY'S MANTRA

_____

TOP PRIORITIES

☐ _____

☐ _____

☐ _____

TO-DO LIST

☐ _____

☐ _____

☐ _____

☐ _____

☐ _____

☐ _____

☐ _____

☐ _____

☐ _____

☐ _____

☐ _____

MEMO

DAILY REFLECTION

MONTHLY PLANNER

MONDAY	TUESDAY	WEDNESDAY	THURSDAY	FRIDAY	SATURDAY	SUNDAY

GOALS

NOTES

MONTHLY PLANNER

MONDAY	TUESDAY	WEDNESDAY	THURSDAY	FRIDAY	SATURDAY	SUNDAY

GOALS

NOTES

MONTHLY PLANNER

MONDAY	TUESDAY	WEDNESDAY	THURSDAY	FRIDAY	SATURDAY	SUNDAY

GOALS

NOTES

MONTHLY PLANNER

MONDAY	TUESDAY	WEDNESDAY	THURSDAY	FRIDAY	SATURDAY	SUNDAY

GOALS

NOTES

MONTHLY PLANNER

MONDAY	TUESDAY	WEDNESDAY	THURSDAY	FRIDAY	SATURDAY	SUNDAY

GOALS

NOTES

MONTHLY PLANNER

MONDAY	TUESDAY	WEDNESDAY	THURSDAY	FRIDAY	SATURDAY	SUNDAY

GOALS

NOTES

MONTHLY PLANNER

MONDAY	TUESDAY	WEDNESDAY	THURSDAY	FRIDAY	SATURDAY	SUNDAY

GOALS

NOTES

MONTHLY PLANNER

MONDAY	TUESDAY	WEDNESDAY	THURSDAY	FRIDAY	SATURDAY	SUNDAY

GOALS

NOTES

MONTHLY PLANNER

MONDAY	TUESDAY	WEDNESDAY	THURSDAY	FRIDAY	SATURDAY	SUNDAY

GOALS

NOTES

MONTHLY PLANNER

MONDAY	TUESDAY	WEDNESDAY	THURSDAY	FRIDAY	SATURDAY	SUNDAY

GOALS

NOTES

MONTHLY PLANNER

MONDAY	TUESDAY	WEDNESDAY	THURSDAY	FRIDAY	SATURDAY	SUNDAY

GOALS

NOTES

MONTHLY PLANNER

MONDAY	TUESDAY	WEDNESDAY	THURSDAY	FRIDAY	SATURDAY	SUNDAY

GOALS

NOTES

Monthly Budget

Income

Income-1		
Income-2		
Other Income		
	Total Income	

Expenses

Month

Budget

Bill To Be Paid	Due Date	Amount	Paid	Notes
	Total			

Monthly Summary

Total Income	Total Expenses	Difference

Notes

Monthly Budget

Income			Expenses
Income-1			Month
Income-2			
Other Income			Budget
	Total Income		

Bill To Be Paid	Due Date	Amount	Paid	Notes
	Total			

Monthly Summary

Total Income	Total Expenses	Difference

Notes

Monthly Budget

Income			Expenses
Income-1			**Month**
Income-2			
Other Income			**Budget**
	Total Income		

Bill To Be Paid	Due Date	Amount	Paid	Notes
	Total			

Monthly Summary

Total Income	Total Expenses	Difference

Notes

Monthly Budget

Income			Expenses	
Income-1			Month	
Income-2				
Other Income			Budget	
	Total Income			

Bill To Be Paid	Due Date	Amount	Paid	Notes
	Total			

Monthly Summary

Total Income	Total Expenses	Difference

Notes

Monthly Budget

Income			Expenses
Income-1			Month
Income-2			
Other Income			Budget
	Total Income		

Bill To Be Paid	Due Date	Amount	Paid	Notes
	Total			

Monthly Summary

Total Income	Total Expenses	Difference

Notes

Monthly Budget

Income			Expenses	
Income-1			Month	
Income-2				
Other Income			Budget	
	Total Income			

Bill To Be Paid	Due Date	Amount	Paid	Notes
	Total			

Monthly Summary

Total Income	Total Expenses	Difference

Notes

Monthly Budget

Income			Expenses	
Income-1			**Month**	
Income-2				
Other Income			**Budget**	
	Total Income			

Bill To Be Paid	Due Date	Amount	Paid	Notes
	Total			

Monthly Summary

Total Income	Total Expenses	Difference

Notes

_____
_____
_____
_____
_____

Monthly Budget

Income			Expenses	
Income-1			Month	
Income-2				
Other Income			Budget	
	Total Income			

Bill To Be Paid	Due Date	Amount	Paid	Notes
	Total			

Monthly Summary

Total Income	Total Expenses	Difference

Notes

Monthly Budget

Income			Expenses	
Income-1			**Month**	
Income-2				
Other Income			**Budget**	
	Total Income			

Bill To Be Paid	Due Date	Amount	Paid	Notes
	Total			

Monthly Summary

Total Income	Total Expenses	Difference

Notes

_____
_____
_____
_____
_____
_____

Monthly Budget

Income			Expenses	
Income-1			Month	
Income-2				
Other Income			Budget	
	Total Income			

Bill To Be Paid	Due Date	Amount	Paid	Notes
	Total			

Monthly Summary

Total Income	Total Expenses	Difference

Notes

Monthly Budget

Income			Expenses
Income-1			Month
Income-2			
Other Income			Budget
	Total Income		

Bill To Be Paid	Due Date	Amount	Paid	Notes
_____	_____	_____	_____	_____
_____	_____	_____	_____	_____
_____	_____	_____	_____	_____
_____	_____	_____	_____	_____
_____	_____	_____	_____	_____
_____	_____	_____	_____	_____
_____	_____	_____	_____	_____
_____	_____	_____	_____	_____
_____	_____	_____	_____	_____
_____	_____	_____	_____	_____
_____	Total	_____	_____	_____

Monthly Summary

Total Income	Total Expenses	Difference

Notes

_____

_____

_____

_____

_____

_____

Monthly Budget

Income			Expenses	
Income-1			**Month**	
Income-2				
Other Income			**Budget**	
	Total Income			

Bill To Be Paid	Due Date	Amount	Paid	Notes
	Total			

Monthly Summary

Total Income	Total Expenses	Difference

Notes

MONTHLY GOALS

MONTH :

FOCUS

GOAL

ACTIONS STEPS

GOAL

ACTIONS STEPS

GOAL

ACTIONS STEPS

TASK LIST

_____
_____
_____
_____
_____
_____
_____
_____
_____
_____
_____
_____
_____

NOTES

MONTHLY GOALS

MONTH :

FOCUS

GOAL

ACTIONS STEPS

GOAL

ACTIONS STEPS

GOAL

ACTIONS STEPS

TASK LIST

_____
_____
_____
_____
_____
_____
_____
_____
_____
_____
_____
_____
_____

NOTES

MONTHLY GOALS

MONTH :

FOCUS

GOAL

ACTIONS STEPS

GOAL

ACTIONS STEPS

GOAL

ACTIONS STEPS

TASK LIST

_____

_____

_____

_____

_____

_____

_____

_____

_____

_____

_____

_____

_____

NOTES

MONTHLY GOALS

MONTH :

FOCUS

GOAL

ACTIONS STEPS

GOAL

ACTIONS STEPS

GOAL

ACTIONS STEPS

TASK LIST

_____
_____
_____
_____
_____
_____
_____
_____
_____
_____
_____
_____
_____
_____

NOTES

MONTHLY GOALS

MONTH :

FOCUS

GOAL	TASK LIST

ACTIONS STEPS

GOAL

ACTIONS STEPS

NOTES

GOAL

ACTIONS STEPS

MONTHLY GOALS

MONTH :

FOCUS

GOAL

ACTIONS STEPS

GOAL

ACTIONS STEPS

GOAL

ACTIONS STEPS

TASK LIST

NOTES

MONTHLY GOALS

MONTH :

FOCUS

GOAL

ACTIONS STEPS

GOAL

ACTIONS STEPS

GOAL

ACTIONS STEPS

TASK LIST

_____
_____
_____
_____
_____
_____
_____
_____
_____
_____
_____
_____
_____

NOTES

MONTHLY GOALS

MONTH :

FOCUS

GOAL

ACTIONS STEPS

GOAL

ACTIONS STEPS

GOAL

ACTIONS STEPS

TASK LIST

_____
_____
_____
_____
_____
_____
_____
_____
_____
_____
_____
_____
_____
_____

NOTES

MONTHLY GOALS

MONTH :

FOCUS

GOAL

ACTIONS STEPS

GOAL

ACTIONS STEPS

GOAL

ACTIONS STEPS

TASK LIST

_____
_____
_____
_____
_____
_____
_____
_____
_____
_____
_____
_____

NOTES

MONTHLY GOALS

MONTH :

FOCUS

GOAL

ACTIONS STEPS

GOAL

ACTIONS STEPS

GOAL

ACTIONS STEPS

TASK LIST

_____

_____

_____

_____

_____

_____

_____

_____

_____

_____

_____

_____

NOTES

MONTHLY GOALS

MONTH :

FOCUS

GOAL

ACTIONS STEPS

GOAL

ACTIONS STEPS

GOAL

ACTIONS STEPS

TASK LIST

_____
_____
_____
_____
_____
_____
_____
_____
_____
_____
_____
_____

NOTES

MONTHLY GOALS

MONTH :

FOCUS

GOAL

ACTIONS STEPS

GOAL

ACTIONS STEPS

GOAL

ACTIONS STEPS

TASK LIST

_____
_____
_____
_____
_____
_____
_____
_____
_____
_____
_____
_____
_____

NOTES

To-Do List

- [ ] _____
- [ ] _____
- [ ] _____
- [ ] _____
- [ ] _____
- [ ] _____
- [ ] _____
- [ ] _____
- [ ] _____
- [ ] _____
- [ ] _____
- [ ] _____
- [ ] _____
- [ ] _____

- [ ] _____
- [ ] _____
- [ ] _____
- [ ] _____
- [ ] _____
- [ ] _____
- [ ] _____
- [ ] _____
- [ ] _____
- [ ] _____
- [ ] _____
- [ ] _____
- [ ] _____
- [ ] _____

Notes & Doodles

To-Do List

- [ ] _____
- [ ] _____
- [ ] _____
- [ ] _____
- [ ] _____
- [ ] _____
- [ ] _____
- [ ] _____
- [ ] _____
- [ ] _____
- [ ] _____
- [ ] _____
- [ ] _____
- [ ] _____

- [ ] _____
- [ ] _____
- [ ] _____
- [ ] _____
- [ ] _____
- [ ] _____
- [ ] _____
- [ ] _____
- [ ] _____
- [ ] _____
- [ ] _____
- [ ] _____
- [ ] _____
- [ ] _____

Notes & Doodles

To-Do List

☐ _____
☐ _____
☐ _____
☐ _____
☐ _____
☐ _____
☐ _____
☐ _____
☐ _____
☐ _____
☐ _____
☐ _____
☐ _____
☐ _____

☐ _____
☐ _____
☐ _____
☐ _____
☐ _____
☐ _____
☐ _____
☐ _____
☐ _____
☐ _____
☐ _____
☐ _____
☐ _____
☐ _____

Notes & Doodles

To-Do List

- [ ]
- [ ]
- [ ]
- [ ]
- [ ]
- [ ]
- [ ]
- [ ]
- [ ]
- [ ]
- [ ]
- [ ]
- [ ]
- [ ]

- [ ]
- [ ]
- [ ]
- [ ]
- [ ]
- [ ]
- [ ]
- [ ]
- [ ]
- [ ]
- [ ]
- [ ]
- [ ]
- [ ]

Notes & Doodles

BILL PAYMENTS

MONTH OF

DUE DATE	BILL	AMOUNT	PAID
		TOTAL	

BILL PAYMENTS

MONTH OF

DUE DATE	BILL	AMOUNT	PAID
		TOTAL	

BILL PAYMENTS

MONTH OF

DUE DATE	BILL	AMOUNT	PAID
		TOTAL	

BILL PAYMENTS

MONTH OF

DUE DATE	BILL	AMOUNT	PAID
		TOTAL	

BILL PAYMENTS

MONTH OF

DUE DATE	BILL	AMOUNT	PAID
	TOTAL		

BILL PAYMENTS

MONTH OF

DUE DATE	BILL	AMOUNT	PAID
		TOTAL	

BILL PAYMENTS

MONTH OF

DUE DATE	BILL	AMOUNT	PAID
		TOTAL	

BILL PAYMENTS

MONTH OF

DUE DATE	BILL	AMOUNT	PAID
		TOTAL	

BILL PAYMENTS

MONTH OF

DUE DATE	BILL	AMOUNT	PAID
	TOTAL		

BILL PAYMENTS

MONTH OF

DUE DATE	BILL	AMOUNT	PAID
		TOTAL	

BILL PAYMENTS

MONTH OF

DUE DATE	BILL	AMOUNT	PAID
		TOTAL	

BILL PAYMENTS

MONTH OF

DUE DATE	BILL	AMOUNT	PAID
		TOTAL	

Bill Checklist

Year : ....

✔	MONTH	AMOUNT	ITEM
☐	JAN		
☐	FEB		
☐	MAR		
☐	APR		
☐	MAY		
☐	JUN		
☐	JUL		
☐	AUG		
☐	SEP		
☐	OCT		
☐	NOV		
☐	DEC		

Shopping List

NO.	ITEM LIST	QUANTITY

NOTES

-
-
-

Shopping List

NO.	ITEM LIST	QUANTITY

NOTES

-
-
-

Shopping List

NO.	ITEM LIST	QUANTITY

NOTES

-
-
-

Shopping List

NO.	ITEM LIST	QUANTITY

NOTES

-
-
-

Shopping List

NO.	ITEM LIST	QUANTITY

NOTES

-
-
-

Shopping List

NO.	ITEM LIST	QUANTITY

NOTES

-
-
-

Shopping List

NO.	ITEM LIST	QUANTITY

NOTES

-
-
-

Shopping List

NO.	ITEM LIST	QUANTITY

NOTES

-
-
-

GOAL TRACKER

MAIN GOAL

ACTION STEPS

1 :

2 :

3 :

4;

GOAL 2

ACTION STEPS

1 :

2 :

3 :

GOAL 3

ACTION STEPS

1 :

2 :

3 :

GOAL 4

ACTION STEPS

1 :

2 :

3 :

GOAL 5

ACTION STEPS

1 :

2 :

3 :

GOAL TRACKER

MAIN GOAL

ACTION STEPS

1 :

2 :

3 :

4;

GOAL 2

ACTION STEPS

1 :

2 :

3 :

GOAL 3

ACTION STEPS

1 :

2 :

3 :

GOAL 4

ACTION STEPS

1 :

2 :

3 :

GOAL 5

ACTION STEPS

1 :

2 :

3 :

FINANCIAL GOALS

FINANCIAL GOAL

TAME FRAME

STEPS TO TAKE

FINANCIAL GOAL

TAME FRAME

STEPS TO TAKE

Financial Goal

My Goal:

Starting Balance:

Motivation

Required Number:

Due Date:

Per Day:

Per Month:

Notes

Savings Goal

Date	Amount

Total:

Goal:

Start Date:

Deadline:

Savings Tracker

SAVING FOR	START	END	GOAL

DATE	MEMO	WITHDRAWAL	DEPOSIT	BALANCE

Savings Tracker

SAVING FOR   START   END   GOAL

DATE	MEMO	WITHDRAWAL	DEPOSIT	BALANCE

SAVINGS TRACKER

SAVING FOR	START	END	GOAL

DATE	MEMO	WITHDRAWAL	DEPOSIT	BALANCE

SAVINGS TRACKER

SAVING FOR	START	END	GOAL

DATE	MEMO	WITHDRAWAL	DEPOSIT	BALANCE

SAVINGS TRACKER

SAVING FOR

AMOUNT

START DATE

END DATE

SAVINGS TRACKER

SAVING FOR

AMOUNT

START DATE

END DATE

Yearly Review

YEAR

TOP ACCOMPLISHMENTS

HIGHLIGHTS

SETBACKS

THINGS TO LEARN

THINGS TO CHANGE

START

STOP

CONTINUE

NEXT YEAR PRIORITIES

DEBT SNOWBALL CALCULATOR

STARTING DATE	MONTHLY SNOWBALL AMOUNT	EXT. PAYMENT IN THE BEGINNING

DEBT	DEBT	DEBT	DEBT
BALANCE	BALANCE	BALANCE	BALANCE
MINIMUM PAYMENT	MINIMUM PAYMENT	MINIMUM PAYMENT	MINIMUM PAYMENT
INTEREST RATE	INTEREST RATE	INTEREST RATE	INTEREST RATE

Month	Date	Payment	Balance	Payment	Balance	Payment	Balance	Payment	Balance

Debt Snowball Worksheet

DEBT		
AMOUNT OWED		
MIN PAYMENT		
EXTRA		
SNOWBALL PAYMENT		

Debt Snowball Worksheet

DEBT		
AMOUNT OWED		
MIN PAYMENT		
EXTRA		
SNOWBALL PAYMENT		

Debt Snowball Worksheet

DEBT		
AMOUNT OWED		
MIN PAYMENT		
EXTRA		
SNOWBALL PAYMENT		

DEBT TRACKER

Debt :

Balance :

Min. Payment :

DATE	PAYMENT	BALANCE

Debt :

Balance :

Min. Payment :

DATE	PAYMENT	BALANCE

Debt :

Balance :

Min. Payment :

DATE	PAYMENT	BALANCE

Debt :

Balance :

Min. Payment :

DATE	PAYMENT	BALANCE

DEBT TRACKER

Debt :

Balance :

Min. Payment :

DATE	PAYMENT	BALANCE

Debt :

Balance :

Min. Payment :

DATE	PAYMENT	BALANCE

Debt :

Balance :

Min. Payment :

DATE	PAYMENT	BALANCE

Debt :

Balance :

Min. Payment :

DATE	PAYMENT	BALANCE

DEBT TRACKER

Debt :

Balance :

Min. Payment :

DATE	PAYMENT	BALANCE

Debt :

Balance :

Min. Payment :

DATE	PAYMENT	BALANCE

Debt :

Balance :

Min. Payment :

DATE	PAYMENT	BALANCE

Debt :

Balance :

Min. Payment :

DATE	PAYMENT	BALANCE

DEBT TRACKER

Debt :

Balance :

Min. Payment :

DATE	PAYMENT	BALANCE

Debt :

Balance :

Min. Payment :

DATE	PAYMENT	BALANCE

Debt :

Balance :

Min. Payment :

DATE	PAYMENT	BALANCE

Debt :

Balance :

Min. Payment :

DATE	PAYMENT	BALANCE

Debt Payment Tracker

MIN. PAYMENT :   TOTAL PAYMENT :

PAID	BALANCE	PAID	BALANCE

Debt Payment Tracker

MIN. PAYMENT :   TOTAL PAYMENT :

PAID	BALANCE	PAID	BALANCE

No Spend Challenge

1	2	3	4	5
6	7	8	9	10
11	12	13	14	15
16	17	18	19	20
21	22	23	24	25
26	27	28	29	30

No Spend Challenge

1	2	3	4	5
6	7	8	9	10
11	12	13	14	15
16	17	18	19	20
21	22	23	24	25
26	27	28	29	30

No Spend Challenge

1	2	3	4	5
6	7	8	9	10
11	12	13	14	15
16	17	18	19	20
21	22	23	24	25
26	27	28	29	30

No Spend Challenge

1	2	3	4	5
6	7	8	9	10
11	12	13	14	15
16	17	18	19	20
21	22	23	24	25
26	27	28	29	30

No Spend Challenge

1	2	3	4	5
6	7	8	9	10
11	12	13	14	15
16	17	18	19	20
21	22	23	24	25
26	27	28	29	30

No Spend Challenge

1	2	3	4	5
6	7	8	9	10
11	12	13	14	15
16	17	18	19	20
21	22	23	24	25
26	27	28	29	30

CPSIA information can be obtained
at www.ICGtesting.com
Printed in the USA
BVHW010835310522
638499BV00013B/210